the neighborhood T.M.

IN COLOR

the neighborhood
T.M.
IN COLOR

by Jerry Van Amerongen

Andrews and McMeel
A Universal Press Syndicate Company
Kansas City • New York

ISBN: 0-8362-1846-9

Library of Congress Catalog Card Number: 88-83865

First Printing, April 1989
Second Printing, January 1990

One can do just so much with pasta.

Bill Chambers has the mental power to make socks fall down.

Barry Scribner's therapist has
a lot of work to do.

The tiny dog's tenacity surprised Samuel.

Little Eddie's last significant heist
was a Big and Tall Men's Shop.

Phylis and her brothers take so many walks
together, her shoes are like new.

Elizabeth journals her way through another relationship.

Richard uses positive reinforcement to stay well clear of ear infections.

Have you ever wondered why top executives have such strong toes?

Skipper's beginning to have trouble
with his sense of smell.

"Am I doing my dance at the very periphery
of life's stage?!" Tom wondered.

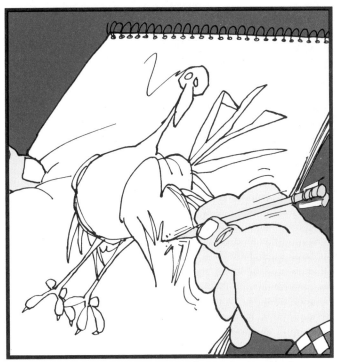

Billy messes up his drawing of a leopard.

James exudes intimacy at a muted pitch.

Victor has a knack for booking the wrong conventions.

Willard began Gracy's driving lesson with "release the hand brake,"
but followed it with nothing of substance.

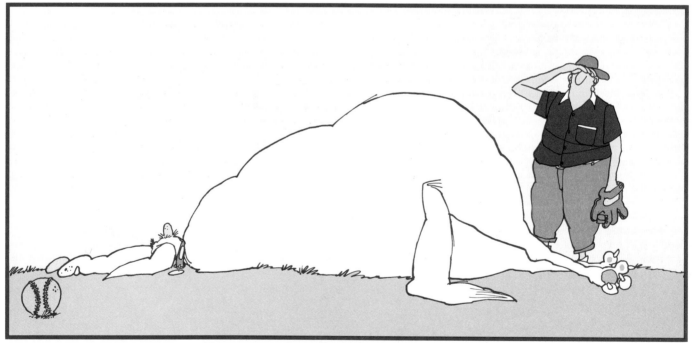

Your pet may have limitations as a play-partner.

Top executives hope to induce more effective decision-making
by greatly increasing the flow of blood to their brains.

When the brain gets conflicting messages.

Ex-Blue Angel, Arnie Tibbets,
is starting to get bored.

Another high-performance thought
for Nordstrom.

Store owner Artie Brodrick could see the sign already.
In big red letters, it would read "No Loose Devices in the Store."

It's all Al can do to give life the
benefit of the doubt.

The villagers trace their unusual custom to
the beastly cold winter of 1573 and one
Eric The Bald.

"Wouldn't a good flea powder
be more efficient, Basil?!"

Billy is what you might call an
imperceptible tease.

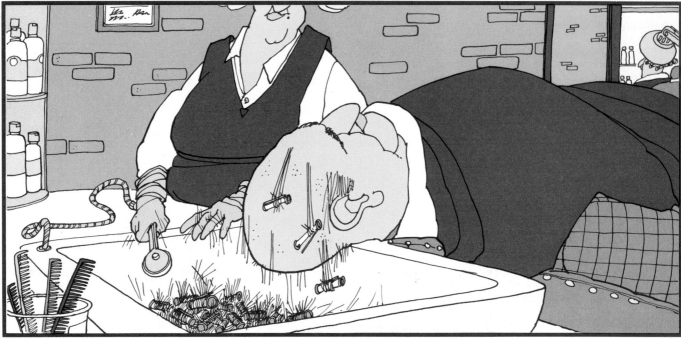

Robert's perm didn't take.

"Look, Allen, the clouds are upside down.
No wait, we're upside down."

Wayne has not gone unaffected by
his years of commuting.

Lewis suffers another telekinetic power outage.

Marcia misses the point of another play.

A sense of wellness spread over the others, as Allen was introduced
to the rest of the problem-noses encounter group.

The power of advertising.

Years later, Brian would make real progress in therapy, only after
he remembered his mother made all of his clothes in grade school.

Sorting through old photographs, Gordon comes across
the origins of his motion sickness.

Calm self-assurance lies just beyond Carl's peripheral vision.

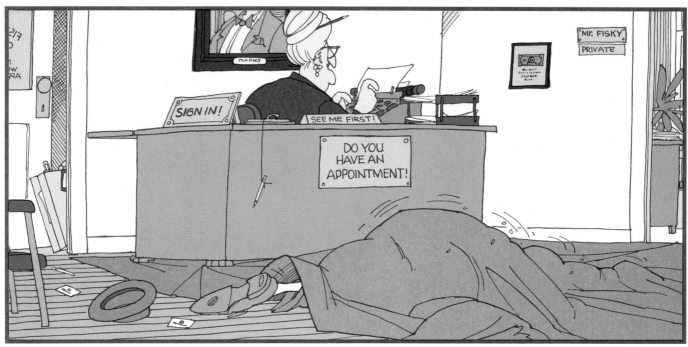

Super salesman Murray Slaughter makes another cold call.

Behold the drama of man and his environment.

Celia breaks the logjam of immobility.

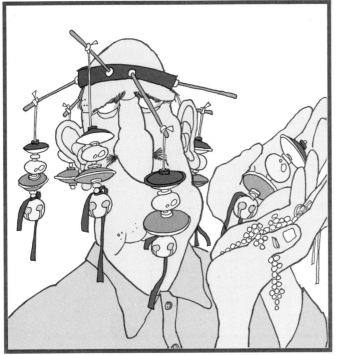

Gerald is in the midst of a creative crisis.

"There goes one of the senior people now."

On weekends Uncle Carl and Aunt Emma traveled to small towns,
where they masqueraded as Naval Reservists.

Warren's having trouble with Dixie Cups again.

"Oh, what the heck. Let's have another apple!"

How the brain works.

Mr. Gregory facilitates Bob's search
for greater opportunity.

A fellow member of our flock performs
his mating ritual.

Canoeist from Hell.

"I'm gonna buy me the same kind
of fertilizer next year!"

Cynthia's view of life is in soft focus.

Skippy suffers an attack of co-dependency.

A man who's obviously in business for himself.

The stranger may not have been wearing a gun,
but he was trouble just the same.

"Are we having steak again?" asked Marshall
in his peevish and wholly irritating manner.

Charles spends a bug-free
afternoon on the patio.

This wasn't exactly what Ben had in mind.

Mr. Starky leans more towards conflict than conflict resolution.

Mrs. Harky always fidgets when Charles chooses to walk to work.

As the official lagoon diver for Gordie's Polynesian Emporium,
Carlos retrieves condiments accidentally bumped from waterfront tables.

Another thing the realtor didn't mention.

There's quite a story behind the Berry brothers' bait shops.

This should put a stop to all that talk about the "Old Man"
being able to withstand the board's challenge.

During a rendition of "Here Comes the Sun," cause-and-effect-oriented
set designer Berry Darnell weaves his magic.

Big Norm Kasner is as intense a spectator
as he was a competitor.

Richard's pain threshold is so low he screams
when he puts on after-shave.

Poor Mrs. Tweed. She has no idea
Mr. Hooper's brain tells him to undress
completely after three drinks.

Harold Stang made a mental note to check
all materials coming from this product
manager's area.

Derek got a "D" in his small-engine repair class.

Viewing houseboat water ballet from a difficult angle.

At 3:30 A.M. the guy in the next room manages to get his
bathroom faucet to make a steady high-pitched whine that is
almost but not quite beyond human hearing.

How they stir their oatmeal, down at the lab.

Kevin was the first of the picnickers to misuse his watermelon.

"I really do wear cheap clothes," thought Richard.

Ernie knows how to torment his wife.

"Thank you very much ladies and gentlemen!
And now we'd like to do a Pink Floyd medley..."

Virginia was disappointed to learn her personal
color was "putty."

The judges remain unimpressed.

When President Tibbs delivered his annual
remarks to the board, the cause of the
company's aimless drift surfaced.

Another family system in disarray.

Eric solves the week-old mystery of
his son's missing fish bait.

Preston seems unaware of the
boundaries of others.

"Ladies and gentlemen, Mr. Bolt Upright!"

Another thing about answering machines is that you also know which call you didn't get.

At last night's party, the Dorseys' dog fell in love with a coat.

Eddie's spending way too much time with the mouse.

Although outwardly placid, this neighborhood conceals
a hotbed of Spider-People activity.

Even though she received a harsh and unforgiving performance review,
Connie still took the time to admire her boss's socks.

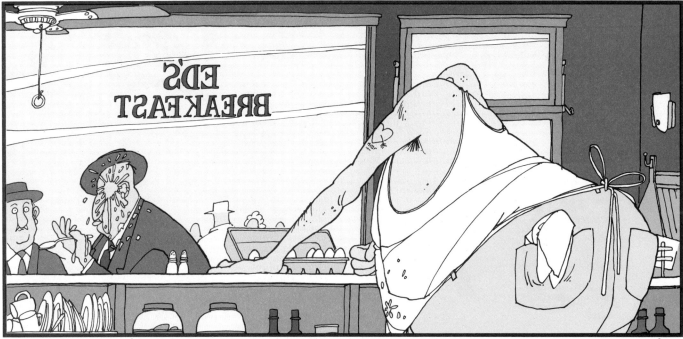

Hardly a negative critique escapes Ed.

Biffy's bark is worse than his bite.

The Tripp Brothers continue
to parlay their name.

Virgil no longer circulates efficiently
within the herd.

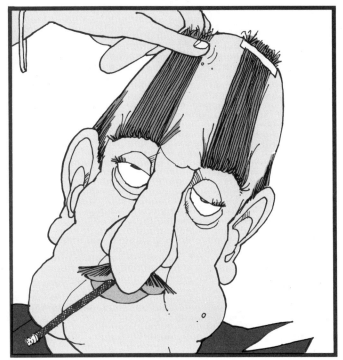

Gavin toys with the possibility.

Marcia was picked on unmercifully all the way through high school.

Graham's journey toward self-mastery is slowed.

Archie has yet to come to terms with his body.

Business.

The hard part is getting the proper length rope,
as Mrs. Nummer well knows.

HAVE YOU FORGOTTEN, GILES?! ...THE HENDERSONS' DOG ATTACKED YOU THE LAST TIME YOU WORE THE FLOWERED TIE!...

Julian leaps into life with Fervor and Zeal.

Carl anticipates a cleansing opportunity.

Believing Mr. Ornsbey was actually open to his suggestions, Philip is again betrayed by his overly optimistic nature.

It looks like Arnold and his dog Fluffy are gonna do a little dusting today.

Dentist Aaron Bixby (who also holds a degree in veterinary medicine) gets confused while demonstrating how to maintain really white teeth.

Just now Geraldine's mind is doing the equivalent of a square dance.

It took a while, but Leon figured out where to lay off his anger.

It took a heated strategy session and a trendy restaurant to draw out Philip's true feelings.

Foreman Bud Harger's presentation at the weekly production meeting
represents 17 years of yeast leaching into his system.

Raymond's just spent his 2½-hour lunch sitting
directly over an air-conditioning duct.

Some of Philip's behavior is directed from
far below his conscious level.

At home with an efficiency expert.

Mrs. Starkey thanks Neal for being her neighbor for the second straight year.

The new guy next door brings a certain symmetry to Graham's life.

Mrs. McGurky always calls out her fruit.

Given as he is to self-deception, Phil thought he had handled
the stairs rather nicely.

Mr. Hadley is sorely lacking in people skills.

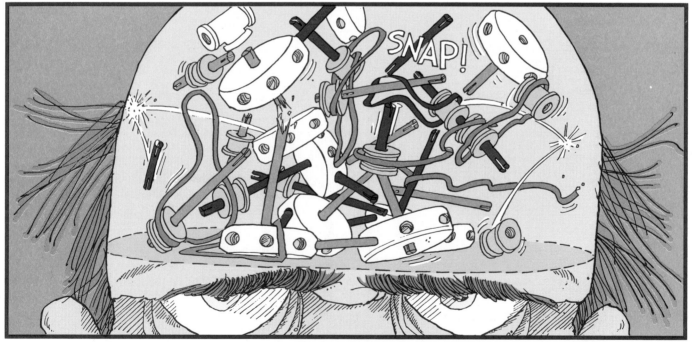

The third martini.

Everett belongs to the Marshall County Miniature Ropers Association.

Michael is a book collector with very little interest in self-help books.

Shirley has no way of knowing she'll return as a frog in her next life.

Arlene begins to lose Garrett during the final stages of their loan application.

William's train of thought makes all the stops.

"Folks, I'm afraid I'm going to have to collect your spoons."

Skipper sensed there were those who wished to have
him believe it was night . . . But why?! . . .

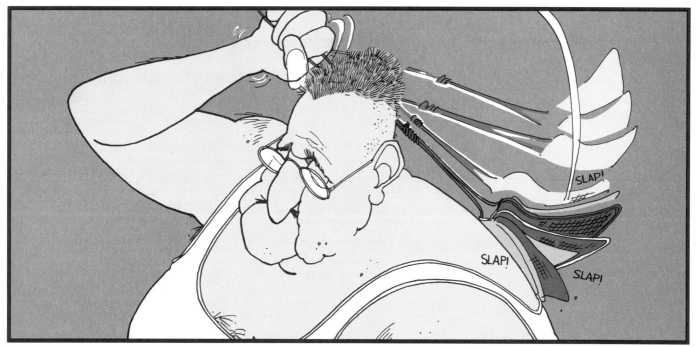

No, this is not a guilt-free day for Francis.

Marie takes another unsettling drive with her
ventriloquist husband, Russell.

THE NEW AGE: Another good thing about becoming a clairvoyant,
is that you can usually fit in aspects of your old job.

Beginning next year, officials of the Miss Gurkey County pageant will
more closely scrutinize the talent program of prospective contestants.

Boyd could almost taste the sale.

Once he reaches the office, Bob's day
is all downhill.

Max reads only decent, manly books.

"All right, all right! I'm not the easiest guy to live with!"

For Clifford, the voice of reason speaks in muted tones.

Entrepreneur Berrie Scubbs looks over the landscape of life with the eye of a backhoe operator.

Once every month or so Norman Banks parks his personal enhancement
kiosk at the local shopping center.

A little soul-searching's in order before Farrell
attends another meeting of his
lighter-self group.

It was the suddenness of the gift that made
Elizabeth appear ungrateful.

Helen employs a new method
of conflict resolution.

Samuel pursues his interest in sleep deprivation.

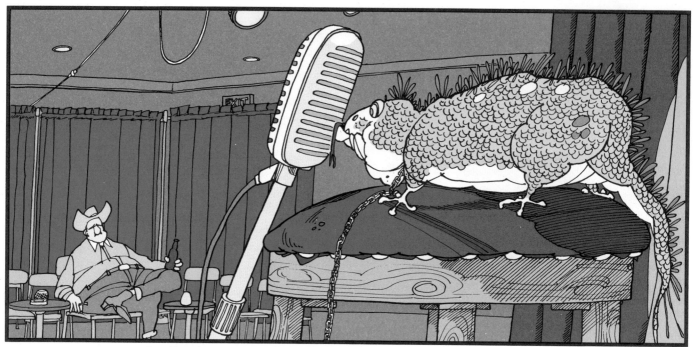

Another low moment in lounge entertainment near Midland, Texas.

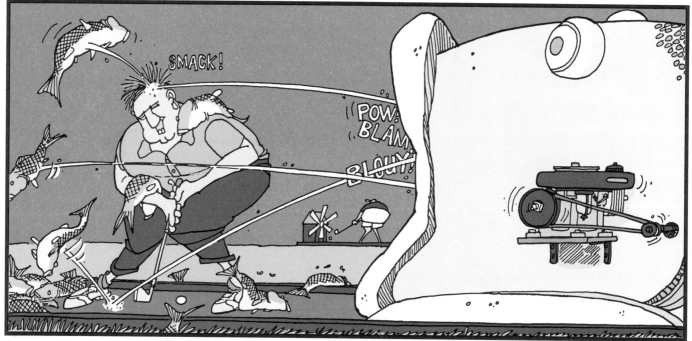

The third-toughest miniature-golf hole in the country.

Larry Toussaint and his patron Mr. MacPherson.

Gregory is a sucker for a southpaw.

Florist Nathan Carlisle uses potting soil to discourage would-be muggers.

Mr. Bob, master of the improv.

Once again we're reminded of the interdependency of our species.

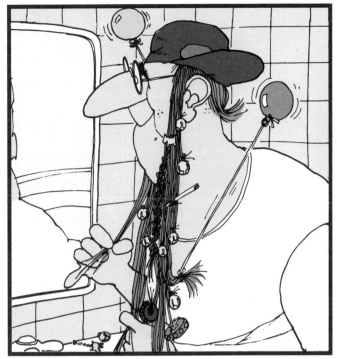

It's probably just as well Carl never had
any corporate aspirations.

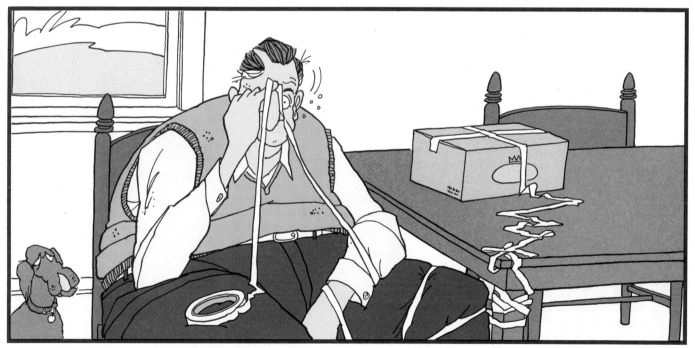

For a few moments, Pierre's brain lapses into chaos.

Tony's the kind of guy who looks for bulky items,
just so his garbage bags fill quicker.

Capt. Richards identifies his escape maneuver as the "Ralneck Spin,"
which carries a hefty 5.2 degree of difficulty.

"Phyllis, step over here for a minute."

What happens when our brain makes us stare.

Another family system gone haywire.

Aaron manages to combine a belligerent
lifestyle with a love for electric trains.

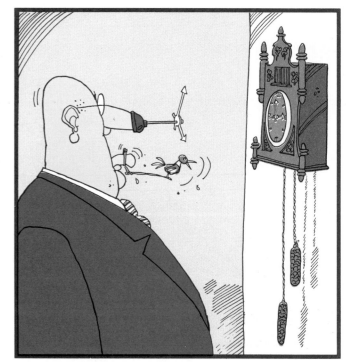

Meanwhile, Mrs. Burfy is taking steps to have
the clock removed from the house.

Philip sits in his amusement room.

Mr. Bigalow waits just so long for service.

It's easy to see why Gene always gets picked
to watch for the bus.

It seems Mr. Pringly's Great Dane has decided
against joining this evening's exercise!…

And so, within Sandra, the vestiges
of her oldest child upbringing stir.

Brian is largely insensitive
to Claudia's proximity.

As esprit de corps fades.

The neighbors stay low-profile with the insecticides
when the Spittle twins are around.

Time to move along, thought Bob.

Top management actually looks forward to the
Annual Shareholders Meeting.

The selection of Neil Keiser as host was a mistake waiting for air time.

Exit Mel Sweeney of Mel Sweeney's Crepe Paper Surprise
and Boutique.

Bubbles and the Prince of Darkness.

Actually, Elliot only drinks to numb the effects
of life on his friend, Paul.

Gary wears false eyes to confuse predators.

"Bob, see that Annexco's acquisition team doesn't get into this meeting until I get H.C. out of the muskrat suit."

Arthur has taken to dropping large, inexpensive fish on people's shoes.

This is the photo that pretty much closed the
Glenn Archer School of Retriever Training.

Fred displays another aspect of his chameleon-like personality.

The weekend starts badly for Lowell.

Bob and Shirley's relationship is troubled
by an imbalance in the distribution of need.

A secret society called The Formation of the Vowels.

Mr. Efficiency, Cliff Sanders, had his sign
tattooed on his head.

Gregory has a fear of being painfully gummed
by pan fish.

Paul is stopped by the Silly Police.

Winnowing and sifting, winnowing and sifting.

Bob loses his footing on Flat Back Rock near Pratfall, Arizona.

Lyle is the product of a cheap ventriloquist school.

Mr. Herrington is menaced by
an electronics bully.

The saga of Harold (Hard Luck) Hadley
continues.

The backyard's rich topsoil is beginning
to come between Ted and Ginger.

Eric contemplates a possible snafu
down at the toaster factory.

Through the use of disguise, Virgil hopes to avoid
compliance with the new leash law.

Fred drinks a lot of milk.

Carl loves the idea of merging.

It was disconcerting to Professor Murray when James
dressed up for voice lessons.

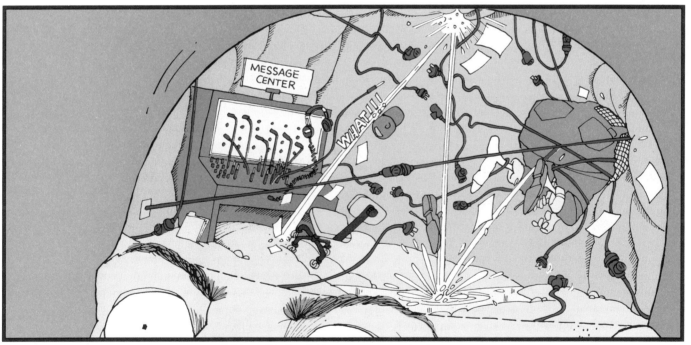

How the brain jumps to conclusions.

Looking north towards Slack Jaw Falls.